Unfuck Your Anger

USING SCIENCE TO UNDERSTAND FRUSTRATION, RAGE, AND FORGIVENESS

FAITH G. HARPER,
PhD, LPC-S, ACS, ACN

MICROCOSM PUBLISHING
Portland, Ore

UNFUCK YOUR ANGER
Using Science to Understand Frustration, Rage, and Forgiveness

Part of the 5 Minute Therapy Series
© Dr. Faith Harper, 2016, 2020
This edition © Microcosm Publishing, 2020
First edition, first published 2016
Second edition, first published Jan 10, 2020

ISBN 978-1-62106-338-4
This is Microcosm #337
Illustrations by Trista Vercher
Book design by Joe Biel

For a catalog, write or visit:
Microcosm Publishing
2752 N Williams Ave.
Portland, OR 97227
www.Microcosm.Pub

Use this book alone or with the accompanying workbook, now in its second edition.

To join the ranks of high-class stores that feature Microcosm titles, talk to your local rep: In the U.S. **COMO** (Atlantic), **ABRAHAM** (Midwest), **BOB BARNETT** (Texas/Louisiana/Oklahoma), **IMPRINT GROUP** (Pacific), **TURNAROUND** (UK), **UTP/MANDA** (Canada), **NEWSOUTH** (Australia/New Zealand), **GPG** in Asia, Africa, India, Latin America, Middle East, or **FAIRE** and **EMERALD** in the gift trade.

Did you know that you can buy our books directly from us at sliding scale rates? Support a small, independent publisher and pay less than Amazon's price at **www.Microcosm.Pub**

Library of Congress Cataloging-in-Publication Data

Names: Harper, Faith G., author.

Title: Unfuck your anger : using science to develop a healthy relationship with frustration, rage, and forgiveness / Dr. Faith Harper, PhD, LPC-S, ACS, CAN (author).

Description: Portland, Ore. : Microcosm Publishing, [2020] | Summary:
"If you've ever been so pissed off that you did things that you regretted, or ruined your own day and some other people's too, this book is for you. Or if you feel angry every single day and it's affecting your health and sleep and love of life. Or if you've got very good reasons to be mad as hell, and you aren't going to take it anymore. Or if you've repressed your anger all your life and now it's all coming out at once. Microcosm Publishing bestseller Dr Faith explains here what the hell is going on in your brain and how to retrain yourself to deal with enraging situations more productively and without torpedoing your relationships. This is Your Brain on Anger gives you a heady dose of neuroscience and cultural explanation of what anger is and what it does to you, and then gives you a handy four-step checklist to help you deal with maddening situations after (or before) the fact, guidance on getting over things, and a chapter on forgiveness. Your brain actually knows what it's doing, and anger can be a good thing sometimes--just not if it's ruining your life"-- Provided by publisher.

Identifiers: LCCN 2019021974 | ISBN 9781621063384 (paperback)

Subjects: LCSH: Anger. | Emotions.

Classification: LCC BF575.A5 H3457 2020 | DDC 152.4/7

LC record available at https://lccn.loc.gov/2019021974 Library of Congress Control Number:2019942377

MICROCOSM · PUBLISHING

MICROCOSM PUBLISHING is Portland's most diversified publishing house and distributor with a focus on the colorful, authentic, and empowering. Our books and zines have put your power in your hands since 1996, equipping readers to make positive changes in their lives and in the world around them. Microcosm emphasizes skill-building, showing hidden histories, and fostering creativity through challenging conventional publishing wisdom with books and bookettes about DIY skills, food, bicycling, gender, self-care, and social justice. What was once a distro and record label started by Joe Biel in a drafty bedroom was determined to be *Publisher's Weekly's* fastest growing publisher of 2022 and has become among the oldest independent publishing houses in Portland, OR and Cleveland, OH. We are a politically moderate, centrist publisher in a world that has inched to the right for the past 80 years.

Global labor conditions are bad, and our roots in industrial Cleveland in the 70s and 80s made us appreciate the need to treat workers right. Therefore, our books are MADE IN THE USA

CONTENTS

Introduction

Nothing pisses me off more than being angry.

Pun intended, obviously, but in all seriousness? I really do hate myself for getting angry. It feels awful. I don't like that rush of feeling activating my body. I worry that I will fall out of control. That I will turn into the kind of person who hurts others. The kind of person who has hurt ME in the past.

I've had over a decade of mindful meditation practice. I've worked in mental health even longer than that. I feel like I should have transcended anger by now, though I know that it doesn't work that way. On the other hand, I do think that awareness in and of itself is what has best prevented me from letting my anger hurt others and myself.

Most everyone has been irritated by their own anger, right? I'm not alone in this. And while we've all seen some ridiculous, unreasonable, pissed-off person in action and thought *"And HERE is the problem with the world,"* most of the anger we deal with day in and day out is not that person raging on the evening news, or the person who loses their shit in the middle of the grocery store parking lot. In reality, there aren't *that* many of those over-the-top, out-of-control pissed off people out there (although it feels like it some days).

In reality? Most angry people? Are just . . . us.

Normal, everyday people who are not walking around the world with a chip on their shoulder labeled "entitlement." Instead, we're normal everyday people who are just in a lot of pain. People who are overwhelmed by what is going on in our lives or in the world at large, and are responding to these feelings of disempowerment by trying to reclaim some sense of agency. People who weren't allowed the vulnerability of "softer" emotions like sadness and fear, so they sublimated it into anger. People who grew up in households that were so violently angry that they have never seen anger used as anything other than a weapon of abuse. And people who struggle against feeling angry in general, trying desperately not to react with anger, either towards others or toward ourselves.

One of the questions I get all the time is this:

"When is anger a valid emotion?"

And the answer is the easiest one ever.

Always.

That's because anger isn't the problem.

And if right now you are thinking something along the lines of *"Yeah, I've had my nose broken by someone else in the past so fuck off with telling me anger isn't a problem."* I get that. And also? Me, too. But the other person's anger wasn't the problem. The problem lay in how their anger was weaponized against you.

How we utilize that anger is what matters. Feeling and acknowledging anger isn't something to be avoided. We don't have to suppress our anger to keep from reacting in harmful ways.

Having a better understanding of anger has the potential to help you in many facets of your life.

In physics there is something called the *observer principle*. This refers to the phenomenon of how simply observing something has an effect on it. The minute you start watching something, the thing that you are watching changes. If you are going to watch some cells on a slide under a microscope, you turn the microscope light on, right? And the cells are going to react to that light.

The same is true of our own emotions. Once we start paying attention to our feelings, thoughts, and physiology we are already starting to make huge changes in how they affect us and how we interact with the world. We are shining a light on our own internal shenanigans. Those big shifts in emotional health start with flipping the light on.

Being a therapist who understands anger doesn't mean I don't ever get angry. Nor does being in therapy. Nor does being a Buddhist. Or just being someone who continuously works on my shit, as exhausting as it is to do so. Maybe some people transcend . . . but I'm not one of them and I don't think I'm remotely close to being one of them. But all of those identities have helped me observe my anger differently so that I don't weaponize it into harmful action. And I'm happy with that result. So I'm sharing what I know.

In this book, we are going to discuss the common triggers of anger, using some new research on the brain's rage circuits. Then we are going to look at what happens in our body when we have an anger response. After the science-y part of what anger is, we're gonna do the unfuckening part. We're gonna go through all those light-shining activities that help us understand our unique and personal anger responses, and discuss how to channel our anger into better relationships or barnstorming social action. And I'm gonna share all the work I've done in my life around learning how important forgiveness is for my own-damn-self. We are going to discuss ways of living with our very real and valid anger responses without losing our shit or swallowing our rage like so much poison. Because if feeling anger is OK, you can *be* angry and still be OK.

Another important note: I'm going to talk a lot about how anger is a *response*. Not just to situations and other emotions . . . but also in connection with other emotional health issues. And because that is true, it means we can't talk about anger without talking about the possibility of underlying mood disorders or anxiety disorders. And because I've written books on those subjects, some of the information from those books have been revisited in this one. Not to be that asshole who is padding her book with lots of fluff and bullshit, but because I hate nothing more than when an author says, "Hey you should go buy my other five books to really understand this shit."

If you've read my other books, you're already good to go on all the brain science. But if you've never seen all the science of how mental health issues affect the nervous system and the like, I want to make sure you have those basics available in the context of anger. One of my life rules is "don't be a dick" and it would be a dick move to send you on an information scavenger hunt to really get what's going on with anger.

There's also a ton of exercises in this book that can help you out as well. Y'all keep telling me you like having stuff to *do* because you are all about the self-accountability. That's bad-ass, right there. So there's *lots* of stuff to do. So much so, that besides the exercises included in this book, there is a whole other anger workbook that you can get go go along with this one if you dig it (and no, you don't need to buy/have both for the book to make sense . . . which refers back to the rule of no dick moves).

Still with me? Let's do the thing.

IRRITATION

FRUSTRATION

MAD

FURIOUS EXPLOSIVE RAGE

This is Your Brain on Anger

What is Anger?

Anger isn't an on or off emotion. That is, we don't flip a switch from calm to enraged. Anger exists on a continuum. The low end may have us feeling irritated, annoyed, or frustrated; a mid point of irate, upset, or pissed off; and a boiling point of furious, enraged, or eruptive. Anger is the encompassing term for all of these activating emotional states that are *driving us to action.* Just like every other emotion, what we call "anger" is just our brain's interpretation of our bodies' biochemical reactions.

All emotions are information, designed to help us make decisions that will protect us and keep us safe. They are formed in the middle part of our brain, in our amygdala, based on the information we are processing and our memories of past situations.

The emotions that we think of as positive are a type of "carry on" feedback. These are when our brains are telling us "Yes! Yes all cookies! Yes hiking with friends! Yes funny movies! These things feel nice, let's do all these things!"

Then there are the emotions that don't feel good, the ones we consider negative. They are the cat scrunched up in the corner, ears flattened and growling. "No! Do not want! Does not feel good or safe or nice at all! Make it stop!" Fear, sadness, jealousy, shame. And, duh, anger. Anger is a huge one, right?

When we perceive something at a conscious or subconscious level as a "threat" (and more on what we've evolved to consider as threats in a minute), our bodies release adrenaline (epinephrine is the more science-y term, it's all the same hormone though) from the inner part of the adrenal gland. That's the *adrenal medulla* if you want to sound really cool at parties.

The adrenals are designed to help us cope with stress (which will sound familiar if you have read my books on depression and anxiety) . . . which means that anger is the label our brains give to certain circumstances that activate our stress response. Adrenaline, in biology-speak, is a *nonspecific* hormone, meaning it acts all throughout the body. It relaxes our airways so we stay oxygenated, but keeps our blood vessels contracted, so the heart and brain keep up the supply of oxygenated blood needed to react quickly and decisively. That means our hearts start pounding, our breathing gets more rapid, our muscles tense up, and our brain goes, *"Oh! We're angry! Got it!"*

We have brains equipped for more primitive survival that aren't intuitively adapted to the modern age. Technology has evolved faster than humans, so we have bodies adapted for simpler times. Instead of hunting, gathering, cuddling, and napping, we are crossing more terrain on a daily basis, interacting with more people, and taking in far more information than we are built to manage. It's a continuous overload.

In recent years, we've learned to understand the neural circuitry of anger as one of those vestiges of what we needed to survive in our not-really-that-distant human history. And like other evolutionary changes, this is another one that is incomplete—just like the ability to digest lactose after age three.

There is a serious biological basis for our anger. It's not a matter of being weak willed or morally deficient. Certain cues in the environment fire off a very specific survival response in the body.

Anger triggers the sympathetic nervous system. It pushes us into survival model . . . which we call the *fight/ flight/freeze response.*

Fight is *beat their ass before your ass gets beat.*

Flight is *get the fuck up out of here this isn't safe.*

And freeze is *if you play possum and don't respond at all maybe all this will go away.*

And this is crazy important to our survival. This whole process is our emergency broadcast system, replete with electronic beeping in the background.

The prefrontal cortex takes in some outside information. Like someone bumping into us (physical attack or dumbassery?), our backpack not being where we left it (stolen or misplaced?), or a friend not showing up for plans and not responding to messages (ghosting us or stuck in traffic?) The amygdala flips through the index of previous similar experiences and if the shittier option was the one that panned out it says, "I REMEMBER THAT! LAST TIME THAT

SHIT HAPPENED, IT HURT! HURT SUCKS!" And the brain stem tells the prefrontal cortex "GET THE FUCK UP OUT OF THERE! WE DON'T LIKE TO HURT!"

So we say "Peace out, threatening situation, gotta jet!" Or we fight back. Or freeze up and play dead and hope the situation passes us over.

The presumption is that an anger response provokes the fight response. But that isn't necessarily true. The fight/flight/freeze response is a *survival response*, not a *dominance response*. Which means that our brain is doing some background calculation of how to best survive the threat it has detected. We fight if fighting is our best chance for survival, but fleeing the situation may make more survival sense. And there is lots of evolutionary evidence that freezing is also a great protective response if we can't overwhelm or outrun our attacker. It numbs the pain of attack, and sometimes confuses the attacker into thinking we're already dead, therefore, uninteresting. You see this in the animal kingdom all the time—an already-dead animal won't be eaten because it may be rotten. The predator then loses interest and moves on allowing the prey to escape.

You may be thinking "Erm, question?" and raising your hand right now. Metaphorically, in your mind of course, so you don't look weird in the middle of the coffee shop in which you are reading this book. "If I have a flight or freeze response how can I call that anger? Isn't it fear or anxiety or whatever else instead?" you are asking, because you are a super-great question asker and that's a really relevant question.

Remember that "anger" is an emotional label the brain comes up with to explain the activation of the stress response. You can still be angry and have a flight or freeze response. And you can absolutely be angry and identify other emotions (fear, anxiety, etc.) along with the anger. Bear with me on this one. I promise it will make way more sense when we get into evolutionary rage circuits plus all the theory on anger as a secondary emotion and the like. Anger is in not just about having your fight face on.

Emotions are pretty good at a lot of things, but they overgeneralize like motherfuckers. Our amygdala is not the highest-functioning portion of the brain. It often likes to send positive emotions about things that aren't particularly good for us. (Cookies are great but *all* the cookies? Not so much.) And it often likes to send negative emotions about things that aren't putting us in actual danger.

All emotions are just information from the body propelling us to attend to what's going on around us and help us determine how to react. This is a good thing. All emotions are good things. Even the sticky, shitty, gross-feeling emotions are good things. They are the "this is what's up" of our place in the world . . .

. . . when they are reactions to the present moment.

When fucked up shit happens, we encode those experiences as *episodic autobiographical memories* or *EAM*. Situations that remind of past fucked up shit activate our survival responses so we don't get hurt again.

Our ability to have a strong response to EAM memories is actually a huge evolutionary advantage for humans to a certain extent. The brain remembers the past and presumes it's the future and emotes accordingly (anger, anxiety, fear, etc.) to get us to pay attention.

In modern society, this evolutionary advantage has become a hindrance. The past should absolutely inform our present, but it generally doesn't serve the present. When we were hurt in the past, and it continues to bubble up in the present, it's our primal brain playing the same cassette tape on a loop. And this emotional state (again, anger, anxiety, fear, etc.) prevents constructive action because it isn't in response to a present threat. Or it just becomes the thing we do because we don't know what else to do with the memories we are living with. EAMs activate an emotional response based on the notion that "it's better to be safe than sorry."

So short answer? When someone is an immediate threat (real or perceived) to you or someone you love, anger will propel your ability to protect what's important, right?

There's one important caveat here: Remember how I said that anger is a survival response, not a dominance response? When anger occurs naturally, that's true. But some people use anger in a willful, conscious way to get what they want. Uncontrolled anger versus manipulative anger can be differentiated by how the angry person reacts when they get their way. If they are still upset after their demands are met, it wasn't a conscious domination tool. If they calm down the minute they are appeased, it was. That's a diagnostic trick that therapists use to see if someone has an anger problem or a coercive control problem.

Getting to Know Our Rage Circuits

Our brains have something called *rage circuits*: predispositions to react with anger when something threatens us and activates our adrenaline. "Snapping" isn't a rare thing at all, but rather a very normal part of being human.

And research now bears out the things that activate the rage circuitry. The researcher R. Douglas Fields has identified nine rage triggers in the human brain and made created the mnemonic LIFEMORTS that covers all of the ones that have been identified

Anger responses are automatic in the face of these nine triggers. Most situations that provoke anger involve more than one. Researchers are now mapping each one individually. They all fire off differently in the brain, so we can see in a literal way how the different rage circuits fire off in the brain, activating our stress hormones. Which means this isn't a theoretical listing of anger triggers, but categories based on our evolutionary survival instincts.

Life or Limb – This one is pretty obvious, right? All animals, including humans, will defend themselves if they perceive an attack against them as life threatening. The brain's wiring is designed to say "Hey, you are prolly gonna die right here so kicking ass is probably your only way out. And even if you can't, you at least won't go down without a fight."

Insult – In more modern language, this is "disrespect." Insult is what we perceive as happening when something disrupts the social order of things, or if there is an argument about dominance within a group. Whether a ram or a mean girl, all members of the animal world will throw down if they perceive an insult to their status.

Family – We will all protect members of our family from attack. This makes evolutionary sense, right? We can't guarantee the passing down of our genes to the next generation if everyone in the fam is killed off, so this is a hardwired reaction. It's the likely precursor for why we may hate everyone we are related to but will still beat the shit out of anyone outside of the family that messes with them.

Environment – We are all wired to protect our territory. Even my indoor cats will sit in the window and scream bloody murder at any neighborhood cat who happens to cruise through the yard. So when you see your fellow humans getting riled up about the neighbor's dog taking a big, gnarly shit on their grass?

Or someone deeply put out because a co-worker used their desk? It's an environmental trigger.

Mate — Just like the family trigger, the ability to pass down our genetic material is attached to getting and keeping a mate. Even if you aren't procreating with your mate, the brain wiring telling us to protect them is the same, because our mates increase our own chances of survival in the world since we're on the same team.

Order in Society — This trigger exists among all social species, but is more overt in humans because our survival is interdependent—meaning, dependent on our social systems. This is different from the "insult" trigger because it isn't about social dominance, but rather it is about social norms and status quo... keeping the social system solid for the good of everyone who operates within it. People who rock the boat in our society trigger a fear response that everything will collapse around us because what they did wasn't "fair." Meaning it violated the rules that we have designed for our interactions. This is the trigger for both mob violence and social justice movements, which demonstrates exactly how anger can be either horrific or a motivation for great change, depending on how it is harnessed.

Resources — Just like wolves will protect their meal source, humans will go to great lengths to protect their resources. If we consider something valuable property, threats to that property can invoke violence. Not just our box of hot Krispy Kreme donuts, but our money, our favorite shoes, and the family photos we hang on the wall are all our resources.

Tribe — Again going back to our need for interdependence, humans, in particular, will defend "their" people against outsiders. This is the essential "us versus them" trigger that isn't about passing on our genetic material, but our need to protect our group from other groups. Contact with competing groups connects to the other LIFEMORTS triggers (resource depletion, threat to mates or family, etc.) because historically, resources were consistently scarce (and for many people in the present, still are). Border walls are not a new debate, human history is replete with walls and moats designed to protect the people we designate as our own. Religious wars are based in this anger trigger. Racism is based in this trigger. Gang violence and military invasions are based in this trigger. Understanding and managing this trigger is essential to human peace.

Stopped – All animals, humans included, will fight against restraint. Any time our will or progress is subverted by another and we are blocked from our movement as free people, we will respond with anger. This is why people can really lose it while being stuck in a long line. It's a response to what is in our way. This is also a trigger (like the order in society trigger) that can become the impetus to fight back against systemic oppression. Where the Order in Society trigger is about agreed upon norms, the Stopped trigger is about expression of free will. Once oppression against an individual or group is recognized as a restraint from having the same benefits of others in society, individuals and groups will fight back against the oppressor.

Plenty of other things can make our response to rage-circuit activation far more dangerous. There are three big issues to take into consideration when remembering that we are primitive brains and bodies bopping around in a modern world.

- All the drugs that we take (whether prescription drugs or street drugs) are altering our circuitry. I'm not even talking about synthetic opioids and antipsychotics. Even just the steroids we take to treat breathing issues or that rash that won't go away change our brain.

- We are constantly inundated with tons of information and misinformation through the little computers that live in our pockets, information that is shaping our worldview and fostering a sense of overwhelment.

- We have weapons of greater destruction than our ancestors did. People with quick-trigger rage circuits did far less damage with rocks and fists. And I'm not just referring to semi-automatic rifles . . . think of the damage we can do just with the vehicles we drive. Or even just the availability of tall buildings on every corner of every city, allowing us the impulse of shoving people off of them or down the stairs of them.

Dr. Fields discusses road rage as an excellent example of how the weirdness of modern society butts up against our more primitive brains. Road rage is common, though rage at people moving around you in a crowded shopping mall or on a hiking trail isn't. If we are walking and someone walks in front of us, we perceive them as walking through the same environment we are, rather than impeding on an environment that is ours, not shared. But if another car cuts us off, it can trip the environmental LIFEMORTS trigger, just like if someone broke into our house, because we have created a territory trigger around our car.

We all, by nature of being uniquely ourselves, react to triggers in different ways based on our personal wiring, our past life experiences, and whether or not our responses are heightened by some of the modern adaptations of society mentioned above.

This brings us back to the observer effect. Once we start to recognize our rage circuits firing off we can deal with them in a different way, hopefully preventing shitty behavior or horrible tragedy.

If the first step of changing something about ourselves means recognizing what's going on, it is a far more effective exercise to do so in a thoughtful way. This worksheet helps you recognize your emotional labels around anger, the effect they have on your thinking patterns and physical reactions, *and* gives you space to recognize your LIFEMORTS triggers. So if you have certain triggers that are particularly apparent, you can plan to deal with them more proactively, right?

Here's a formula for thinking about your rage triggers. (There's a worksheet to fill out for this in the *Unfuck Your Anger Workbook*, if you're into that.)

- What angry emotion did you feel? (Irritability, frustration, annoyance, rage?)

- What thoughts were associated with the emotion?

- What body sensations did you feel?

- Which LIFEMORTS triggers do you think were at work?

The AHEN Model

While anger may be the first emotion we recognize in ourselves, and the emotion we act (or react) upon, I guarantee you it actually isn't the first thing you feel in any given situation. Anger is a response to a deeper emotion. It's a secondary emotion, meaning it's *reactive*. Not just to situations we encounter but to other emotions.

The best model I have seen to explain anger uses the acronym AHEN. The LIFEMORTS model helps us figure out what evolutionary rage circuit is getting tripped in us. Understanding our physiology is important shit. But the primary therapeutic tool I use with clients is this one because it's about attending to our underlying emotional processes once a rage circuit is activated.

AHEN is as simple a conceptualization as you can get.

Anger emerges from

Hurt

Expectations not met

Needs not met

Of course, it is a little more complicated than that in that we aren't usually limited to just one of these underlying experiences but a big glob-ball of two or all of the above a good deal of the time.

Here's how to use AHEN. Next time you are pissed as all get-out, ask yourself the following questions:

Am I hurt? Did something happen here that made me feel insecure? Unsafe? Unvalued? Unworthy? Unappreciated? Just plain sad as fuck? Of all the things that have kicked me in the nuts over the years, why is this situation particularly nasty? Was it the person who I perceive as doing the hurting? Is it a particular situation that bothers me more than others? Has this been a problem for me in the past? Is this one of those fucking *triggers* people yammer on about?

Break this shit down . . . *why* the hurt?

Did I have expectations that were not met? Was my little brain bopping along expecting a certain thing to happen and it didn't happen? If so, was it a realistic expectation? (Be honest here, mmmmkay????) If it was realistic, is it some life-changing shit when it didn't happen?

For example: Someone took the parking spot you got to first. Dick move. Reasonable expectation that they would follow civilized parking lot protocol? Fuck yeah. Otherwise we are 3 inches away from complete social chaos . . . people need to follow some fucking rules, FFS. But is it life-changing? Not so much. You find another parking spot (eventually) and get parked (eventually). Then, hopefully, you move on.

So break this shit down next. Was it a reasonable expectation to begin with? Did the world fucking end because it wasn't met? Some shit is for-real serious, some isn't. Tell yourself the truth here. Is this an expectation worth getting all hurt over?

Did I have needs that were not met? This is a tough one. Because how do you define what a need really is? If you are Buddhist, you may not think they exist at all, right? On an existential level you are all kinds of right. But on a physiological level, the brain is wired to keep you alive. If something threatens the brain's sense of equilibrium, you are going to activate one of the LIFEMORTS rage circuits.

We need to feel safe. We need to perceive our loved ones as safe. If your brain perceives a threat to you, your sweetie, your kids, your pooch? It's ON. Protect what's important to you! Get MAD!

There are other kinds of safety needs we can't discount. Human beings are hardwired for relationships. Not just romantic partnerships, but community in general. We need the stability of relationships in order to be well. Our brains know this, even when society tells us "You don't need no one but your own DAMN SELF!" That's some bullshit. We live with or around others not because we are overcrowded but because we have to do it to survive.

So with that need comes the need for emotional safety. We need to feel secure and supported in our relationships with other people. We need to have a good idea of what to expect. We need to feel loved. This is about more than some dickwad jacking our lunch out of the break room fridge (although, seriously, fucking really????). This is about our fundamental human need to feel supported by others in the world. We need to know that we are safe with the people we love, that they love us back, and that they are not going to hurt us, at least not intentionally. The anger that kicks us in the ass for the longest happens when that contract gets broken. When the person with whom we most needed to be safe did something that questioned that safety.

We need to stay out of dark alleys at 2AM. We need to get away from the erratic driver swerving next to us on the freeway. But we also need a community of people who love us silly and make us feel secure.

You can see how the LIFEMORTS model explains the switch that gets flipped, but the AHEN model really helps us get to our underlying, more personal experiences of anger.

For example, someone raises their voice in a meeting you are attending. Depending on the type of meeting, who else is attending, and your personal history, almost any

LIFEMORTS trigger could be activated for you: Tribe stuff if your people are there; Stopped stuff if they interrupt you; Order in Society stuff if they speak out of turn in general. Now add to that any possible AHENs. If you felt Stopped, you may experience Hurt, Expectations not Met, Needs not Met. If it was Order In Society, it may just be Expectations not Met.

And someone sitting next to you may get angry for an entirely different reason. And the person sitting across from y'all may just roll their eyes and say "Oh, that's just Julie. She has no indoor voice and zero chill when she gets excited. She doesn't mean anything, though."

In short? Our experience of anger, the level at which we feel it, what we do with it, and how long it lasts in us is far more tied to our experience than what initially pissed us off to begin with. And if we don't start figuring out where our anger comes from, then we can never really manage it appropriately.

Personalizing Your Anger Experiences with AHEN

Just like with the LIFEMORTS exercise, this exercise is another way for you to observe your underlying patterns related to your experiences of anger. If you were my client we would totally being doing this in office where I'd say, "Tell me about the last time you got really angry?" but, hey, you can do the same work for free on your own. Good deal.

What are the underlying roots of your anger? If you aren't sure, reflect on when you first noticed that you were angry. What was going on around you—sights, smells, noises, people? What were you doing? What were others doing? What were you thinking about? Any particular memories coming up at that time?

- Once you figured out these underlying roots, were they legit or were they more about you and your history than about the present situation?

- If the roots are legit, are they something that need to be addressed or is it one of those bullshit daily life things that just happens? Speeding ticket, fucked up drive thru order, etc.?

- If it needs to be addressed what is the best way to do so? How do you correct the situation with as little disruption as possible?

- What can you do to keep from getting further hurt in the process (physically, emotionally, and mentally)?

- Can you keep the hurt to others minimal (physically, mentally, and emotionally)?

- Does it need to be addressed immediately, or can it wait until you are calmer and feel safer?

- Is there anyone you can talk to that is going to have a healthy, supportive perspective . . . a counselor, friend, mentor, family member? Someone who knows you, loves you, and will totally call you out on your shit if need be.

- After you act (instead of react), then evaluate the results. Did it work? Is this a strategy that you can use again? Are you still angry or are you feeling better and safer now?

How Our Anger Gets Fucked Up

eeling some serious fucking anger is a normal part of being a human being. Losing your shit is not.

As I tell my clients, "you are allowed to *be* crazy, but you aren't allowed to *act* crazy." Being irritated as fuck because someone jacked the parking spot you were waiting for? Totally legit. Going postal over it? Not so helpful. Not so helpful to everyone around you, not so helpful to greater society, and—for purely selfish reasons—not so helpful to you.

When we lose our fucking minds on a regular basis, we are wiring our brains into a constantly heightened state that eventually fries our circuits (and pushes away everyone we love in the process). We program ourselves to always be on the alert, so we react with far greater speed than we used to and perceive more situations as being dangerous, hostile, or threatening. We are constantly jumping at shadows. A stress switch stuck in the on position tells the brain there is a heightened threat going on in the environment, so we are far more likely to react to LIFEMORTS triggers. Things go from being perceived as an irritation to being perceived as a real threat. The emotion of anger turns into a continuous mood of heightened stress response and low-key irritability and leads to anger outbursts on the regular.

And it's not just the LIFEMORTS circuits that put us at risk. If our brains never get to rest and recharge, we start struggling with many other conditions associated with this wiring change. Added up, those conditions are known as *autonomic nervous system dysfunction*. Many common health problems (heart disease, high blood pressure, food allergies) as well as many common mental health issues (depression, anxiety, PTSD) are related to a continued heightened response. That is, a body with its stress thermostat perpetually in the on position.

How do we get stuck "on?" Well, you know I'm gonna say trauma . . . I mean I wrote a whole book about that, *Unfuck Your Brain*. Survival instincts wire us to over-respond in the present based on the shit that has happened to us in the past. But also, everyday stress that we don't have a chance to recover from or practice self-care around sure as fuck doesn't help either.

But also? Anger can also be the frosting hiding a shit-cake of other mental health issues that need recognition in the own right.

When It's More Than Anger

Being really angry a couple of times a week is a shitty situation to be living in. It will have consequences on your life over time and is definitely something that should be attended to. But anger that is wildfire levels out of control? Off-the-charts anger and/or continuous states of anger? These levels of anger are often the expression of other mental health issues.

After all, anger in and of itself doesn't have its own associated DSM diagnosis (the DSM being the *Diagnostic and Statistical Manual* that we use to assign mental health diagnoses). But it is associated with over thirty other diagnoses as one of the primary symptoms. Remember that anger has neurobiological roots as a secondary emotional response. That means we have to talk about how often anger can be more than just anger.

So many of us slip through the cracks in terms of getting accurate diagnosis and care for health issues, especially the ones that are more invisible. In *This is Your Brain on Depression*, I mention research which shows that up to 20% of the people who go to the doctor thinking they have major depression actually have bipolar disorder (and these are the people who know SOMETHING is up, never mind the people who aren't discussing these issues with their doctors at all). At least half the people with bipolar disorder had to see at least three doctors before getting an accurate diagnosis. The amount of time it takes from first seeking help to actually getting efficacious help for bipolar disorder? Ten years on average. And bipolar disorder specifically is one emotional health category where displays of anger aren't quickly recognized as indicative of elevated mood (more on that in a sec).

Add to that the cultural norms many of us face about mental illness. That we grew up in families or in societies that tell us that we are not allowed to experience depression, bipolar disorder, or anxiety. That emotional issues are displays of weakness that cannot be tolerated. Time and attention for mental health treatment is something other people have the privilege of receiving. But not us.

It's important to discuss what kinds of things we need to look for in ourselves and in those we love. And advocate with treatment professionals when we need to. As in "My anger has been getting me in a lot of trouble, and when I was researching it, it seems that I meet a lot of criteria for clinical depression. I want to look at either ruling that out or learn about possible treatment options if it turns out to be accurate." Because nothing is more badass than dumping old toxic messages about mental health treatment and fighting for the care we need.

Anger Masking Anxiety Disorders and Mood Disorders

Approximately a third of people diagnosed with depression experience "anger attacks," meaning they have an intense autonomic stress system response that they felt was inappropriate to the situation at hand. This reinforces the notion that anger is a secondary emotion, doesn't it?

Individuals with mood disorders like depression who present with significant bouts of anger and irritability are also far more likely to have more complicated and harder to treat depression in general. They have more symptoms to treat and their depressive episodes last longer than the people who don't experience a lot of anger and anxiety. Why-so? First, depression expressed as anger has its roots in emotional regulation and rumination. People who struggle with managing their emotions and tend to get mentally stuck on things that have happened to them are the people who are the most likely to express their depression as anger. You may be thinking "I know from depression . . . and depression can't even be chuffed to get up and take a shower, so big explosive temper tantrums? I think not." And that's generally true . . . that low-level continuous, unmanageable irritability is the most common display. But depressed people can also go boom upon occasion. Remember that anger, just like anxiety and depression, is connected to a disrupted stress thermostat. And a wonky nervous system does all kinds of weird shit.

Anger and irritability can also be how manic episodes present in individuals with bipolar disorder. This makes sense, right? Mania is the term we use to describe an elevated mood. It's not necessarily a "fun" elevated mood—it can just as easily be rage. And this is likely one of the reasons that figuring out if someone has bipolar disorder or depression can be so difficult (and a huge part of the reason that I created the tracking log that you are going to find at the end of this chapter in case you are trying to parse this out for yourself).

Likewise, anxiety can also be underlying our expressions of anger. Anxiety is an emotion that we often experience shame for feeling, making it painful to address, so we shift our heightened arousal into an expression of anger because it helps us feel back in control of our emotional state.

Anger, in theory, gets more shit resolved than wringing our hands and worrying . . . at least according to our amygdala.

Research demonstrates that the medications that help manage depression and anxiety don't help manage the associated anger. The only thing that really does is good old therapy and other forms of brain re-training that help people shift their thinking patterns so they don't get stuck in the feedback loop cycle that leads to continued outbursts. Which means that, while the anger tools in this book are still very helpful for your anger management, you will also need outside treatment so you will be in better control of your symptoms so you can do the self-work you are setting out to do.

Symptoms of Depression

What does the word "symptom" mean? Anything that you are thinking, feeling, and doing that are reinforcing problems or stuckness in your life instead of growth and healing.

Dysthymia is probably best conceived as low-grade depression. You function decently well but it takes everything to do so, and all the energy you spend on the basics leave you with little ability to enjoy the stuff that makes being human worth it.

Symptoms of dysthymia can include:

- *Less interest, or no interest, in daily activities*
- *Feeling sad, or down, or just kind of empty*
- *Feeling pretty hopeless about life*
- *Low energy, feeling low-level tired all the time (whether getting sleep or not)*
- *Feeling like you can't do shit right, having lots of negative self-talk or low self-esteem that isn't really related to reality (because while saying you are bad at dunking when you're 4'11" is likely legit, saying you are fundamentally broken, shitty, and unlovable isn't)*
- *Trouble paying attention, concentrating, or making decisions*
- *Anger or irritability (see there?)*

- *Serious decrease in productivity of effective task completion*
- *Avoiding social situations and activities (the ones you would actually like to do in theory, or used to like to do)*
- *Worry, guilt, or shame*
- *Changes in eating (either overeating or not wanting to eat at all)*
- *Changes in sleep patterns (sleeping too much, not sleeping enough, sleeping badly)*
- *Stuck in the past and negative experiences that happened*

An actual diagnosis of major depressive disorder requires that that less interest or lack of interest in stuff you used to really enjoy (clinical term? anhedonia) has been present every day for at least two weeks. This is the big diagnostic feature of depression. Robert Sapolsky calls depression the clinical inability to appreciate a sunset. And everyone I've ever talked to who struggles with depression totally gets that definition. Like, you empirically can understand that the sunset is pretty . . . but you can't experience the pleasure of it.

Other symptoms that are also really, really common are:

- *Loss of interest in all the things fun, excellent, and the point of being human (anhedonia, like I mentioned above)*
- *Low energy/fatigue*

- *Low-level chronic pain*
- *Headaches, stomach pain, or chest pain*
- *Jacked up concentration, difficulty making decisions*
- *Feeling guilty and/or worthless*
- *Sleeping a ton or sleeping for shit (not sleeping at all, or sleeping badly)*
- *Feeling either super restless or really slowed down (like moving underwater or brain wrapped in cotton)*
- *Intrusive thoughts of death (morbid ideation) or suicide (suicidal ideation)*
- *Change in eating habits (and 5% or more change in weight, either up or down, because of it)*
- *Irritability, anger, low distress tolerance*

Symptoms of Bipolar Disorder

People who have bipolar disorder cycle through highs and lows. It's not depression and non-depression, but depression and mania, an intensely elevated mood. It's not necessarily fun and happy—it can also be high agitation, irritability, and anger. Unlike normal levels of elevated emotions, mania takes us over completely. Someone in a manic state really struggles to control their actions because their brains are in overdrive—no passing go, no collecting two hundred dollars.

Seven of the key signs of this phase of bipolar disorder are:

- *Racing thoughts*

- *Talking really fast*

- *Not needing much sleep to function*

- *Being easily distracted*

- *Feeling really restless*

- *Acting impulsively*

- *Being confident in your abilities far beyond your actual skills*

- *Elevated mood (either super high and happy or super angry and irritable)*

- *Making poor decisions/choices, engaging in risky behaviors (like with sex or money)*

- *Break from reality (psychosis)*

Symptoms of Anxiety

Thoughts and feelings:

- *Excessive worry*

- *Rumination (hamster wheel thinking patterns)*

- *Irritability/anger*

- *Irrational fears/specific phobias*

- *Stage fright/social phobias*

- *Hyper self-awareness/self-consciousness*
- *Feelings of fear*
- *A sense of helplessness*
- *Flashbacks*
- *Obsessive behaviors, pickiness, perfectionism*
- *Compulsive behaviors*
- *Self doubt*
- *A sense that you are "losing it" or "going crazy"*

Physical symptoms:

- *Trouble falling asleep or staying asleep*
- *Inability to rest*
- *Muscle tension*
- *Neck tension*
- *Chronic indigestion*
- *Stomach pain and/or nausea*
- *Racing heart*
- *Pulsing in the ear (feeling your heartbeat)*
- *Numbness or tingling in toes, feet, hands, or fingers*
- *Sweating*
- *Weakness*
- *Shortness of breath*
- *Dizziness*

- *Chest pain*
- *Feeling hot and cold (feeling like having chills and fever without running a temperature)*
- *Shooting pains/feeling like you have had an electric shock*

Symptoms of Unhealed Trauma

Trauma is a different mental health issue from depression and anxiety. Depression and anxiety can co-exist with trauma, but we need to recognize and treat trauma as its own separate thing. It can be really helpful to think of PTSD (and other ongoing trauma responses) as injuries to the nervous system. When we have experienced a trauma that we haven't recovered from, our sympathetic nervous system is on a hair-trigger, expecting danger all the time. So everything codes as a LIFEMORTS trigger, and rationalizing through that response becomes increasingly difficult.

A trauma reaction happens when you are reacting to the present as if it's the past. Anger can absolutely be a trauma reaction. If your response to past trauma was a fight response, your anger in the present may be a trauma-triggered response.

And if we are talking about the symptoms of depression, bipolar disorder, and anxiety we also need to talk about the symptoms of an unresolved trauma response (PTSD or otherwise). Meaning, what kinds of symptoms an unhealed trauma reaction may include and what kinds of things operate as a trauma. Keep in mind that the aforementioned DSM is very specific about the kinds of trauma that qualify for a PTSD diagnosis, but life is full of shitty things happening that can code within your brain and body as a trauma and you don't have to qualify for a PTSD diagnosis to receive trauma-informed care.

Reliving the trauma:

- *Feeling like you are reliving the trauma even though it's behind you and you are physically safe*
- *Dreaming like you are back in the traumatic event (or a similar event)*
- *Having a huge emotional response when something or someone reminds you about the trauma. Like freaking the fuck out, even though you are currently safe and/ or lots of physical symptoms (sweating, heart racing, fainting, breathing problems, headaches, etc.)*

Avoiding the memories of the trauma:

- *Doing things to distract away from thoughts or feelings about the trauma, and/or avoiding talking about it when it comes up*

- *Avoiding things associated with the trauma like people, places, and activities. And a lot of times these areas of avoidance get bigger and bigger. Like avoiding a certain street that an accident happened on. Then the whole neighborhood, then driving in a car at all*

- *Needing to feel in control in all circumstances, like sitting in places that feel safest in public places, not having close physical proximity with other people, avoiding crowds*

- *Having a hard time remembering important aspects of the trauma (blocking shit out)*

- *Feeling totally numbed out or detached from everything or just about everything*

- *Not interested in regular activities and fun stuff. Not being able to enjoy shit, even if it should be enjoyable shit*

- *Not being connected to your feelings and moods in general. Feeling just . . . blank*

- *Not seeing a future for yourself, like just more of the same versus things getting better*

Other physical or emotional symptoms:

- *Stomach upset, trouble eating, only craving foods that are sugary (therefore more comforting to a stressed out body)*

- *Trouble falling asleep or staying asleep. Or sleeping a lot but for shit. Either way, feeling fucking exhausted all the time*

- *Not having enough fucks in your pocket to take care of yourself in important ways (exercising, eating healthy foods, getting regular health care, safer sex with chosen partners)*

- *Soothing symptoms away with substances (e.g., drugs, alcohol, nicotine use, food) or behaviors (e.g., gambling, shopping, or dumb endorphin-producing shit like playing chicken with trains)*

- *Getting sick more frequently, or noticing that chronic physical health issues are getting worse*

- *Anxiety, depression, guilt, edginess, irritability and/or anger*

Keep Track of Your Symptoms

Anger, anxiety, and mood disorders don't show up on lab tests. To get help, you'll usually need to get your own damn self into a clinic saying "shit is fucked and I really really need to figure this out and get help" so that someone can help you sort through the shit and figure out what was wrong. If you can create a good record of what's been going on, it can help you connect with a clinician who can ask good questions, clarify information, and help you figure out what treatment and support you need, and hopefully in far less than ten fucking years.

- List the symptoms you're having
- For each symptom, write down its intensity on a scale of 1-10
- For each symptom, how long do you experience it for, on average?
- How many times per week do you experience each symptom?
- How many months or years has this been going on?

Self-Injury as an Expression of Anger

Research shows, time and again, that individuals with elevated levels of internalized anger—anger at the people who have hurt us and anger at ourselves for being helpless in the face of abuse—are the people who engage in self-injurious behavior.

Essentially, self-injury is triggered by the LIFEMORTS "insult" category. This is because abuse perpetrated against us can cause a deep sense of shame and inadequacy.

The official term is *non-suicidal self-injury*, and it refers to behaviors that individuals engage in which cause harm to their bodies without suicidal intent. The most common forms are skin cutting, head banging or hitting, and burning. Self-injury has often been considered something that women do, but in my years of practice I have seen all kind of people engage in self-injurious behavior. Men and more masc individuals tend to engage in the behavior in ways that are not as obvious to the people around them, like taking unnecessary hits while playing sports. Lower key behaviors may include skin picking, hair pulling and the like (the workbook that goes along with this book has a complete list of every self injury behavior I could find in the literature, if you are interested).

There are a lot of theories as to the purpose of self-injurious behavior. There are two common explanations, that actually serve as polar opposites. One is that an individual feels so numb that self-injury helps them feel *something*. The other is that they feel so much, the self-injury is a distraction and relief from their emotions. Can it be different for different people? Sure. But what's most important is unpacking the question of *what happened that caused someone to arrive at a place where self-damage seems like a rational response?*

We don't talk about the "what happened" nearly enough, even though the research has been there for decades. And, simply, the "what happened" is our stories and interpretations of the abuse, trauma, and the insecure attachments that we form when living in these fucked-up conditions—especially when they occur in early childhood. When we are hurt over and over again, but powerless against our attackers, we lash out the only way we can, by hurting ourselves.

The first season of the HBO thriller series *Sharp Objects* focuses on cutting. In one episode, the doctor of a psychiatric facility explains that many of the people who receive treatment aren't even mentally ill in the way others would assume, in that they don't have schizophrenia, bipolar disorder, and the like. He explains that they are people who were hurt greatly, and they have turned that hurt inward, making them far more a danger to themselves than to those around them.

If you have a suspicion that some of your behaviors toward your own body are self-injurious, or if you are realizing that your self-harm behavior is connected to trauma and internalized rage, therapy can really help your healing.

Unfuck Your Anger

I f I did my job right in the first part of this book, the whole feeling a lot of anger thing is starting to make a ton of sense to you. And if there is other shit going on that has made your anger far worse, hopefully you have a plan to get help for it. But understanding the roots of our anger and recognizing and honoring it as a *valid emotion* is only part of the solution.

Anger provides the energy needed for change. Maybe your situation, maybe yourself. But learning to respond to your anger, not react from it, is the key to healthy usage.

Think of healthy anger as a road you are walking. On the left side of the road there is the anger that we don't allow ourselves to feel and express (which makes us sick and ruins our relationships) and on the other side we have anger over-expressed (which makes us sick and ruins our relationships). If you have veered off onto one side, you want to course correct back to the middle, not overcorrect to the other side.

This section is full of anger management exercises if you are looking for a good place to start on your own anger management—tips and tricks that help you be proactive rather than reactive when you become angry. Managing anger in healthier ways, communicating anger in efficacious ways, and doing the difficult work of forgiveness which keeps anger from residing in your body like a continuous poison. All of the exercises here are designed for you to unfuck your reactive patterns, so you can better utilize your responsive patterns . . . therefore staying on the path.

Your Anger Narrative

We all experience anger in different ways. We are the product of our experiences. What has happened to us, what we have witnessed, what we were taught by others. Being more mindful of our own experiences of anger is the first part in recognizing our own unique experiences of anger. And that allows us a better understanding of them (brain science!) and then managing them (therapy hacks!). You can journal out the answers to these questions (or if you like things workbook-y style, it is also in a fill-in-the-blank format in the aforementioned workbook).

- What incident from your past that you have not let go of has the biggest hold on you?

- What situations typically trigger anger for you on a day-to-day basis?

- What does your anger look like (how do you behave when angry)?

- Which of your behaviors fuel your anger and make it worse?

- What sensations do you feel in your body when angry?

- How does your anger affect your day-to-day life?

- How has anger been destructive to your relationships?

- How has it been self-destructive?

- Is there anyone in your past that you learned your anger behavior from? Is there anyone you're either modeling or reacting against?

- In what ways do your anger and pain continue to serve you?

- In what ways do they operate as a barrier?

- What would life be like if you were not still so angry?

- Would working through your anger be worthwhile? How?

How We Handle Anger

There are multiple ways we can handle our feelings of anger, some of which are generally helpful and others that are far more toxic to ourselves and those around us . . . and the differences can be really fucking subtle. Not to mention they can be circumstance-dependent. How you are with your family may be very different from how you are at work, right?

- **Stuffing** – Anger is swallowed and ignored rather than expressed because it is deemed bad, wrong, or inappropriate.

- **Overt Hostility** – This is open antagonistic behavior used in defense of oneself, regardless of the consequence to others. It could include physical violence or verbal antagonism.

- **Covert Hostility** – While not openly hostile, passive-aggressive people look for means to control situations without expressing their true emotions in an open and vulnerable way. Instead, they will manipulate others in subtle ways. Covertly hostile people are masters at mind games.

- **Boundary Holding** – This means expressing what is okay and not okay without disconnecting from others altogether. It requires a level of vulnerability because it means expressing yourself honestly, knowing that the answer may be no.

- **Releasing** – Dropping anger means recognizing that there are forces outside of your control and that your anger does not serve you.

Reactive

Stuffing

Overt Hostility

Covert Hostility

Proactive

Releasing

Boundary Holding

The first three—stuffing, overt, and covert hostility—are reactive, meaning we are operating from a place of being uncomfortable with or overwhelmed by our feelings of anger so we lash out or lash in. This is where most of us operate from. These are the cultural norms . . . the ways of managing anger that we learn from those around us. This habit of not paying attention to what our body is telling us is what causes so many other mental health issues.

The last two—boundary holding and releasing—are practical and proactive means of handling anger. You are not ignoring your amygdala, you are acknowledging the information it is giving you to keep you safe and figuring out what the best course of action is around that information. Is there something you need to act on or is this old stuff coming up?

Holding a boundary means to be assertive rather than aggressive, doing something proactive about the situation that caused your anger response.

Releasing as a means of handling anger is very different from stuffing because you are not trying to pretend the anger isn't there, but instead are doing the work around detoxing your anger. Releasing is an informed practice of realizing that your anger is directed at something about a behavior that you cannot change or a boundary that you cannot enforce. Releasing often requires forgiveness work when our anger and resentment have become a long-standing, unresolvable emotional pattern within ourselves (more on that in the forgiveness chapter).

All of the work in this book is focused on the last two means of handling anger. Because we are going to be emotionally mature badasses who don't let anger control our everything for the rest of our lives, right?

The 90-Second Emotion Rule

Having a healthy relationship with our anger is really fucking hard, I am well aware. One of the things that helps the most? Knowing there is a time limit to every emotion we feel, including anger. Buddhist practitioners have been saying this for thousands of years, and in recent years, science has shown it to be true.

When looking at stroke research, scientists have been able to measure the amount of time an emotion lasts in the brain. It's 90 seconds. Because an emotion is just supposed to be information, it doesn't last—unless we hold onto it.

If we perseverate and fuck ourselves up over every uncomfortable thing we feel, then yeah . . . we stay angry for hours, days, weeks, months, even years. Anger stops being a brief emotion and starts being our everyday mood. Our stress response stays turned on.

And, conversely, if we try to ignore our anger and not feel it . . . it festers under the surface and leaks out at all the wrong-ass moments. Our stress response STILL stays turned on. Have you ever tried to hold a beach ball underwater? Suppressed anger is just like that.

Anger is the signal to activate our stress response in case we need to jump into our animal survival skills. If we just *feel* our anger—if we recognize it and name it—then the chemical response going on in the brain, the system that got the amygdala all fired up to begin with, settles down very quickly.

Because we paid attention to the message it was giving us.

The trick with emotions is to use them just for what they are: Information to take into consideration. Not necessarily to be acted on with our initial impulses—maybe not acted upon at all—just another piece of evidence to consider before you respond.

If you are thinking "easier said than done, bitch," I gotchu. There is a great exercise to practice recognizing the feeling, paying attention to what it's telling you, then releasing it. It's a skill from Dialectical Behavioral Therapy called *riding the wave*. Because as mindfulness instructor and researcher Jon Kabat-Zinn says, "You can't stop the waves, but you can learn how to surf."

Riding the Wave

Think of each emotion as a wave crashing on the shore. Different types of waves can represent different emotions. Some days, the surf may be mild and some days it may be huge and stormy. But we don't have to drown in the waves. And we know that we can't stop them from coming. So we surf. I know, easier said than done. When you are having a strong emotional response, try this exercise. Hell, even better . . . try it now just for practice:

Observe Your Feeling

Get curious about what's going on. Notice it and name it.

Experience Your Feeling

Let the waves come and go. Don't try to block the feeling, push it away, or hold on to it.

Don't forget: **YOU ARE NOT YOUR FEELING.**

Feelings are information. They are something we experience, not something we are. You don't have to act on it. Remind yourself that you have felt different in the past and will feel differently in the future.

Develop an Understanding with Your Feeling

You don't have to become friends, but you can become more comfortable with its existence. Don't judge it as good or bad, just accept its existence. Maybe you can learn to appreciate what it's trying to tell you.

Acknowledging Anger

There is a big difference between acknowledging and expressing anger.

Expressing our anger means to reveal it through action, whether verbal or behavioral.

Acknowledgement means admitting and owning our emotional state. It involves using an "I feel . . ." statement, whether out loud to someone else or to ourselves in a conscious way.

When we are reactive, we express our anger before we are even aware of what's going on. But if we acknowledge its presence first, we are far more likely to handle it in a better way.

Acknowledgement is a way of taking ownership of our emotional state and validating it, while expressing it projects it onto others. Gayle Roselli and Mark Worden, authors of *Of Course You're Angry*, a book about learning to manage anger after substance abuse recovery, talk about it as the difference between "I feel . . ." and "You made me feel . . ."

An example? Mr. Dr. Faith was working from home one day and I was at my clinic. I asked him to do the dishes while I was out. He didn't. Not because he's an asshole who decided "fuck her and the dishes" but because he was writing and forgot. I was uncomfortably pissed. Some people would have been mildly irritated. Some people would have rolled their eyes at his forgetting but not been upset at all. He didn't *make* me feel angry—all he did was forget the dishes. So I had to unpack my own reaction before I picked a really shitty fight with my husband.

The short answer is that I was hurt (AHEN) because my love language is acts of service and so I interpreted him not doing the dishes as evidence of him not loving me. And that's 100% my shit and not his, right?

When you're feeling angry, try the exercises below to help figure out your best options for strategizing how you want to react to the situation that pissed you off. Bonus tip: You can use these tools with any of your emotions.

What Am I Feeling?

Figuring out our LIFEMORTS and AHENs (which is sounding more and more like some kind of militaristic code for a missile launch the further I get in this book) is only the first step. If you aren't used to handling your anger in a proactive way, using a structured tool can be helpful for doing so. I adapted a tool created by Roselli and Worden that you can use with the AHEN model and the LIFEMORTS triggers to decide on options and create ways to handle issues more consciously. (FYI: I've changed it somewhat from their original model because I think the word "why" is the most useless question in therapeutic history.)

In the heat of the moment, but after you've calmed down enough to not tear up this book and throw it across the room or something, answer these questions about what you're feeling:

- What am I feeling?

- What activated me feeling this way? Any LIFEMORTS and AHENs to take into account?

- What could I do about my feeling? What are my options?

- What am I going to do about my feeling? What is my action plan?

Communicating with 'I Statements'
Now here is a great fucking tool for communicating your action plan to resolve your feelings with someone else. You may decide to share these statements with someone. Or you may just be doing internal work around your own anger patterns. Acknowledgement isn't necessarily done in your out-loud voice.

I feel/I felt_____

When _____ happened.

What I want is _____.

The last part—what you want—is important, because it connects back to your original action plan. Our feelings are completely our own, and we shouldn't blame others for them. We can, however, ask them for different behaviors that better respect our boundaries. Or we can change our own interactions to better protect ourselves.

This skill works in regular communication and stays in place even if your convo has leveled up to a conflict. Keeping ownership of your own feelings completely shifts away from the blame game.

Dirty dishes scenario once again: I had all kinds of possible responses. I could have yelled and screamed and refused to cook dinner until he cleaned up. I could have locked myself in the bathroom and cried. All things that I saw modeled in my childhood as appropriate relational responses. Or I could communicate my feelings (and why they were so strong considering the situation) using "I" statements.

I told Mr. Dr. Faith that I was frustrated and hurt (mildly angry with underlying primary emotions) that he forgot to do the dishes. I told him that remembering to do things I have asked him to do is a demonstration of love to me. That I not only like coming home to a clean kitchen, I feel heard and cared for when he follows through on tasks. There was zero percent "you made me feel" in that conversation, and I expressed a clear understanding of the depth of my response. And he has worked hard to become better about following through on stuff that is important to me. Although I did recently threaten him with divorce on Instagram for leaving my cast iron pan soaking in water, but that's a whole other story.

What About When You Didn't?

In therapy-speak, we call these *exception seeking questions*. Meaning, let's look at the times that you didn't manage anger badly. Sometimes the best tools for anger management already lie within you, we just need to figure out how you draw upon those tools on the regular.

- Can you think of a time where you were angry and you didn't let it take you over?

- How did you do it?

- What was different?

- What helped?

How Can You Reframe Your Experiences?

One of the places in which we get stuck is when we frame the story through the lens of how we were the victims of the violence or neglect of others. While those feelings are valid, they impede recovery. Reframing our experience as one in which we survived can dramatically reframe our experience without letting anyone off the hook for the harm they have caused. Once we realize instead of being stuck in the past.

Try re-narrating your experience, placing yourself as the survivor instead of the victim. For example, many people have been abused at some point in their lives. And yes, they were absolutely victims of abuse . . . I'm not blowing sunshine up anyone's ass and pretending that wasn't true. But focusing on our victimhood continues to empower the abuser, years after we are away from them. If we focus on our capacity for survival and the strength it took to do so, it lessens the power abusive people from our past have over our reactions in the present and future.

Something Pissed You Off? Let's SOLVE Your Problem

This tool (adapted from *Dr. Weisinger's Anger Workout Book*) is an even more structured way of mapping out and creating solutions. It helps get your thinking brain back online when your emotional (angry) brain is trying to take over the show.

State Your Problem: Identify and define the problematic situation.

Outline Your Response: After describing the details of your problem as specifically and expansively as you can, then detail your usual response. Researchers who studied expert problem solvers found that they didn't look at the problems in abstract terms, but instead focused very concretely on the "who, what

List Your Alternatives: Brainstorm all your possible solutions. Yes, even "magical thinking" type solutions or "go back to bed and let it figure itself out" solutions. They bubble up, and that's ok. Don't worry about quality, the important thing is quantity. Come up with as many different possibilities as possible.

Visualize Your Consequences: Consider the possible outcomes of all of the alternatives you listed. What might happen in both the short and long term? Are these consequences you can deal with? Cross out anything that is clearly a non-starter. Consider combining alternatives and visualizing how that would work.

Evaluate Your Results: Now you gotta act. Use the same strategy in more than one scenario (you know, on multiple occasions when people piss you off). What are the actual consequences? Is this an improvement over the old ways you responded? Do you need to go back to the drawing board, or do you have a good handle on things now?

Physiological Anger Disruptors

Sometimes riding the wave of anger or coming up with good adulting action plans just isn't enough. You need other ways of calming your physiological anger response in a literal way. If anger is associated with our physical body flipping the on switch, how do we use our bodies to turn it back off? Here are some really great (evidence based!) ones, followed by instructions for a few others that are about 3% more complicated, in case you are worried you might be doing them wrong (though you are quite likely doing just fucking fine ... Mr. Rogers and I both are proud of you for trying your ass off!)

- **Singing:** The neurocircuitry for singing is in the cerebral cortex, therefore disrupting the subcortex fear and threat response. Any singing works, but you can borrow this Acceptance and Commitment Therapy (ACT) trick. Come up with a story of your anger (e.g. "he never listens when I'm talking") in a few words. Then sing it to the tune of the Happy Birthday song. It's so hard to hold onto the anger story when doing so, trust me!

- **Humor:** This adds a complexity to sensory input that disrupts the activation of the fear and threat response. This isn't mean jokes or snark . . . genuine silliness, goofiness, and funnieness.

- **Intentional Breathing Exercises:** These can calm the sympathetic nervous system and get the parasympathetic nervous system back online

- **Mindfulness Meditation:** Hippocampus and prefrontal cortex are activated but the cingulate cortex is not.

- **Mantra Meditation:** Hippocampus and prefrontal cortex are activated but the cingulate cortex is not

- **Yoga, Tai Chi, and Qi Gong:** All of these practices activate the neurons outside of the brain and calm the vagus nerve, putting the body in charge of the brain.

Meditation on the Soles of the Feet

Adapted from a study by Singh, Lancioni, Singh, Winton, Sabaawi, Wahler & Singh (2007)

Good news! No one is going to shave your head and make you wear saffron robes. Meditation, mindfulness, and even mindful meditation is not part of a religious tradition, it really is just about a better understanding of your own experiences in the moment. This particular meditation has been well researched to work with individuals who struggle with anger outbursts, even individuals who were considered "uncontrollable" because of their intellectual disabilities, brain injuries, and the like. I love that this proves that meditation can literally be for everyone.

In terms of setting the scene? This may be a "well, duh" thing to say but the more calm and relaxing the atmosphere, the better. Even if you can just dim the lighting a bit it can really help.

1. If you are standing, stand in a natural rather than an aggressive posture.

2. If you are sitting, sit comfortably with the soles of your feet flat on the floor.

3. Breathe naturally and do nothing.

4. Cast your mind back to an incident that made you very angry. Stay with the anger.

5. You are feeling angry, and angry thoughts are flowing through your mind. Let them flow naturally, without restriction. Stay with the anger. Your body may show signs of anger (e.g., rapid breathing).

6. Now, shift all your attention to the soles of your feet.

7. Slowly, move your toes, feel your shoes covering your feet, feel the texture of your socks or hose, the curve of your arch, and the heels of your feet against the back of your shoes. If you do not have shoes on, feel the floor or carpet with the soles of your feet. Keep breathing naturally and focus on the soles of your feet until you feel calm.

9. Meditate on the soles of your feet for about 10 to 15 min.

10. Slowly come out of your meditation, sit quietly for a few moments, and then resume your daily activities.

Alternative Nostril Breathing Technique

(Sanskrit Term: Nadi Shodhana)

This breathing technique has been shown to calm the body by giving you control of your autonomic function, meaning it literally helps you calm yourself down and has been shown to be more effective for this purpose than other breathing techniques designed for the same purpose (e.g., paced breathing).

To practice ANB, fold your middle three fingers into your palm so only your thumb and pinky finger are extended. This is the universal sign for "call me!" the Hawaiian sign for "hang loose" and my alma mater's sign for our mascot, the roadrunner.

Beep, beep.

Ahem, anyway. Use your thumb to close one nostril and breathe in through the other.

Move your hand to use your pinky to close the other nostril while releasing your thumb from the first nostril to breathe out.

Lather, rinse, repeat.

Chair Yoga

These are all bend-at-the-waist yoga forms that I specifically use to calm the vagus nerve and get the parasympathetic nervous system back online. That's the scientific explanation if you need to scare off anyone at a party. In normal person speak, it means that bending at the waist tells your body to calm the fuck down and stop preparing to fight.

They are all meant to be done seated, to make them more every-body accessible. You can absolutely do these poses on a mat, but a chair can give you some good support, especially if you don't have much yoga experience, have limited mobility, some pain issues, etc. But even in a chair, and even when not doing yoga forms that require extending the arms, you can still end up hurting yourself . . . and yoga is *not* supposed to hurt.

Some rules:

1. Don't do shit that hurts.

2. Modify whatever you need to modify so it doesn't hurt.

3. Don't do these exercises at 100% effort. Allow yourself the experience of only putting in 10% effort. Yoga works just as well (if not better) at 10% effort. Let yourself relax.

4. If you find yourself holding your breath, you're working too hard. You should be breathing because you are a human being and the breathing in and out thing is important, OK?

5. Use a chair that isn't on wheels, has a straight back, and (ideally) does not have arms.

6. Make sure you tell everyone that you totally did yoga today. Bonus points if you are drinking kombucha while you tell them and you finish the convo with a "Namaste."

In keeping with the principles of trauma informed yoga I don't use the Sanskrit names for the yoga forms. And for that matter, I refer to them as "forms" instead of "poses" or "asanas." I also don't include breathing cues in my descriptions and encourage you to experiment with your inhales and exhales as you move through the forms. These linguistic and cuing choices are intentional and evidence-based, informed by the research of David Emerson.

The term *asana* is Sanskrit, therefore isn't known by people outside the yoga community (and folks feel shut down and excluded when they literally don't speak the language). Emerson's research shows that the word "pose" can be triggering for individuals with sexual abuse histories (especially for individuals who had to pose for their perpetrators). He settled on the term "forms" for its neutrality so I use it as well.

You'll also notice I don't specify when to breathe during each pose. This also comes from Emerson's work, specifically with veterans who have been trained to fire their weapons on the outbreath, and found cuing the outbreath to be triggering. Breathe in a way that feels natural for you, and look at how your movements become easier or more difficult if you are breathing in or out while doing them.

Mountain Pose

Sit straight up and extend your spine.

Root down in your chair on the lowest part of your tailbone (your sit bones)—the two points that take the weight of your body when you sit.

Be mindful to keep your legs at a 90 degree angle, with your knees directly over your ankles, with some space between your knees. This is a great pose to simply engage your core, check in with your posture, and focus on your breath. Come to this pose after each of the poses below.

Roll your shoulders back and pull your belly in toward your spine, then relax your arms down at your sides.

Cat-Cows

Keeping both feet on the floor and your spine long, put your hands on the tops of your thighs, or your knees, if you can do so comfortably.

Arch your spine and roll your shoulders toward your back. Moo!

Round your spine, and drop your chin toward your chest, rolling your shoulders forward inward to your chest. Meow!

Continue moving back and forth between cat and cow positions, experimenting with moving during inhalations and exhalations, 5 to 10 cycles.

Sufi Rolls

As you inhale, lean your torso over to the right and then circle it out in front of you and around to the left, coming around the back as you exhale. Create a circle, leading from the belly button. Inhale forward and exhale backward. Then reverse.

Chair Pigeons

Move back into seated mountain, then bring your right ankle up to rest on your left thigh. Keep your knee parallel with your ankle as much as possible and hold this form for 5 breath cycles if you can do so without pain or discomfort. If you want to deepen the stretch, you can bend your waist forward over your leg. Repeat with the left leg.

Seated Forward Bend

Start back in seated mountain form, then fold your upper body over your legs from the waist. You can leave your hands at your sides or use them for extra support in the form by resting them on your thighs, then slide them down your legs as you hinge forward. Experiment with holding this form for 5-10 cycles of breathing. When you are ready, move back into seated mountain form.

Single-Leg Stretch

For this one, you can scooch forward closer to the edge of the chair for more traction (but not so close you end up biffing it, ok?)

Stretch your right leg out, pointing your toes up and resting your heel on the floor. Rest your hands on your right leg, then lift up through your spine and bend over your right leg, sliding your hands down your leg to support your movement forward. You can take the stretch as far as it feels comfortable, but don't push yourself to tshe place of pain. You can hold onto your ankle or the back of your calf for support if you are able to drop that low. Hold this position for 5 breath cycles, if possible, and experiment with deepening the pose as you breathe.

Repeat with your left leg.

SINGLE LEG STRETCH

Final Relaxation Form

Sitting comfortably in your chair, drop all muscle tension. Close your eyes or allow your gaze to soft focus into the middle distance. Focus on your breath and notice sensations in your body. Allow yourself 2-3 minutes of rest before getting up from your practice.

Transforming Anger into Social Action

You may be thinking "Yo, lady, shit is FUCKED UP if you haven't noticed."

I've noticed. I'm with you.

While this book has been very much about our internal work around anger, I would be completely full of shit if I didn't address the fact that horrible fucking things happen in the world every day.

Ongoing, systemic injustice in the world breeds a different sort of anger, doesn't it? The LIFEMORTS and AHENs actually aren't any different, they're just continuously

shit-piled onto one group of people by another in an effort to control our larger culture.

Moral anger is a term that is bandied about and typically ill-defined. Most definitions revolve around being angry about something being morally wrong, which is pretty vague. I think it's better termed as the empathic connection to systemic injustice in the world. The not okay-ness of the individuals most in need of care being the most likely to be hurt. Moral anger, then, is what propels us to shift systemic injustice into systemic change. Moral anger is vital to human survival, but needs to be handled as carefully (or maybe more carefully) than other forms of anger. This goes back to walking the path of anger—recognizing its validity and coming up with a plan that is proactive instead of reactive.

How do we use our anger to effect change on the macro level?

1) **Validate our experience:** Every great vustice change started with the cognitive shift from "That's just how things are" to "This is fucked up." Once we've recognized that shift in ourselves, we can search for others having the same experience. The ultimate goal is for enough people in our community to have the same cognitive shift so we can promote change.

An excellent recent example? When the #MeToo and #TimesUp movement became viral on social media and the depth and breadth of the problem regarding systemic violations of women by men became clear and the issue could no longer be ignored. And that started opening up conversations about how other groups in society are continuously harmed by the larger social norms. A radio show host who had interviewed me in the past and got in a tiff with me about active, continuous consent contacted me and invited me back on his show, saying that the issue obviously needed to be readdressed and he needed to hear me in a different way (which, I need to add, is huge self-accountability internal work on his part). By shifting from irritation and defensiveness, he validated the experiences of the individuals who have been victimized, which lent support to social change.

2) **Own our privilege and power:** We are not the sum of our disenfranchisement, we are the sum of our assets. And our assets are not just our fundamental agents of change, our recognition of them informs our compassion for others and our intersectionality. My friend Naomi Brown, who is a minister and social

worker, calls this conscious using of privilege to help those who do not have it *sneaking in the front door*. Power and privilege lets us get into spaces others could not. This doesn't mean speaking for them, but providing support and amplification of their experiences.

3) ***Know our history:*** Efficacy at change requires understanding the history of change movements. Knowing challenges others have faced, knowing theory of action (which is just a fancy way of saying what works best in producing change with the least chance of furthering harm) gives us tools we wouldn't have otherwise. Reinventing the wheel slows down the process right? You're trying square wheels and triangular wheels before you hit upon round ones working the best. Every social movement has a contextual past that should inform our present and future. It's not enough to just be morally outraged. We need to be morally outraged *and* educated in the work of Franz Fanon, Paulo Freire, Barbara Jordan, Fannie Lou Hamer and other ideological ancestors. You don't have to have a PhD to get started, but seek to center as much knowledge as possible along your journey.

4) **Find the helpers:** To quote Fred Rogers, who was quoting his own mother. In every situation there are people out there helping to make it better. They may not be advocating for the exact same thing that you are determined to fix, but change-seekers will always be your people. They are already activated to do work and have already made connections where connections need to be made. These are your allies and compatriots.

5) **Activate the base:** Change comes from a place of emotionality, not logic. You were activated by your moral anger, right? Emotional safety and security as a key changing point will be far more important than logic when you are trying to shift public opinion. Our rights are stripped away when leaders induce fear in the populace. Witch trials, concentration camps, and bathroom bills are all fueled by fear. Fear isn't rational, so logic doesn't combat it. Only connection does.

6) **Be proactive and strategic:** Rarely do we need to react immediately. I've found that the madder I am, the more important it is for me *not* to react immediately, because I am far less efficacious when I do so. The AHEN model applies to moral anger as

much as it does any other form of anger. I need to pay attention to what it is telling me, then figure out what I need to get the job done. When we look at the civil rights leaders of the 60s, we see this work in action. Rosa Parks is an excellent example. She wasn't just a tired woman who said "Fuck it" and sat down on the bus one day. Rosa Parks became political once she saw how her brother was treated by society after fighting to protect it in World War II. She joined the local chapter of the NAACP and had not only been involved in the organization for twelve years by the time of the incident, but was the chapter secretary. She was chosen as the face of the movement for her impeccable record and reputation. Her protest was planned and, the same day as her arrest, leaflets were dispersed on the doorsteps in African American neighborhoods calling for a bus boycott. "Fuck-its" rarely induce systemic, long lasting change. Planning and organization and capacity building do.

Forgiveness

We all know someone whose health deteriorated after a major, traumatic blow in their life. We've all known people or at least heard stories of people who "died of a broken heart." Or were "never the same again" in both emotional and physical ways after being subject to great hurt.

Forgiveness researcher Dr. Matt James has found over decades of study that the people who are hurt the most are usually the people who are most determined to forgive. I have also noticed this in my own practice. My guess is that at some cellular level, we recognize how much holding on to anger and hurt from the past is damaging our present and future. Or, as Dr. James notes, the more horrible the crime against us, the more we resonate with the truth that forgiveness is a matter of life and death.

So many physical health issues have been correlated with the inability to forgive. The list is endless (increased cortisol levels, autoimmune issues, heart issues, etc.) but essentially, the inability to forgive keeps the body in a chronic state of inflammation. Dr. Candace Pert, a researcher known for her work in psychoneuroimmunology, stated that forgiveness creates a quantum shift in our bodies at a cellular level that frees the energy we need to heal and thrive.

Ok, that sounds all kinds of woo-woo. Let's try putting it another way. Frederic Luskin, the founder and director of the Stanford Forgiveness Project, has a fantastic analogy for describing what's happening when we hold on to our anger past the point of it serving its purpose. He says, envision yourself a police officer. You see someone haul ass past you at 90 miles an hour. You set off to pull them over, but the engine on your squad car fails and you're stuck. Ok, so you write them a ticket and stick it in the glove box or what? And you continue to do that for every violation you see speeding past? You now have a glove box full of unenforceable tickets? What are you gonna do with that mess? You are now drowning in tickets. Since you can't enforce them, you have to continue to contend with them. Do you want to sit around counting and sorting tickets or do you want to use that energy to go do bad-ass, world changing shit?

In other words, forgiveness, done right, is selfish as fuck.

It's about taking your power back. It's about owning your own energy again. It's about making space for something other than pain in your life. *There's nothing wrong with selfish as fuck when it comes to self-care.* Face masks and cold press juices are all good, but forgiveness is the ultimate form of self-care.

That's it. It's not about being a better person or a better practitioner of a particular religious faith. I mean that's cool AF if it happens. But if you go into it with that goal and expectation, you are setting yourself up to fail. And be frustrated. And then have something else to be mad about.

It's also not about eating shit to keep the peace. Or letting others gaslight you about their fucked up behavior. Forgiveness doesn't mean letting people continue to stomp all over your boundaries. Instead, forgiveness takes the emotionality out of a toxic relationship, which helps you establish and maintain more solid boundaries in the future. The angers and resentments you still hold empower the people who have hurt you in the past to control your life in the present because they maintain an energetic link to them. You can think of that in a metaphysical woo-woo sense if you are down for that, or you can just consider it in terms of the energy it takes for you to continue to be angry at someone for shit they did a long time ago. That's a lot of fucking energy going down the drain every day. And fuck that, they don't get to have that much control over you anymore.

How Do You Know There Is Something to Forgive?

It's not always super obvious, is it? Sometimes we think we are over something and then it bites us in the ass. Dr. Luskin has developed a few tells in the course of his research.

- When you remember a past incident, do you have a strong emotional and/or physical response to it? Like some level of reliving the initial pain you were caused?

- Do you find yourself stuck in the story of the event? Like the same thoughts or storytelling (internal or to others) whenever you are activated?

- Do you focus on this negative experience from the past more than you focus on the good in your present? Or even just your life in the present and your goals for the future?

These are all good indicators that you are trapped in a cycle of anger and pain that won't dissipate without some serious forgiveness work. The anger and hurt you experienced when the event took place was an important and valid response. Those feelings are activating to provide you protection at the occurrence, but they aren't beneficial to you in the future.

In other words? *Your baggage does not have to be your identity.*

Types of Forgiveness

Back to Dr. James' forgiveness research. He differentiates *episodic forgiveness* from *trait forgiveness*. Episodic forgiveness refers to the work we do to forgive someone who hurt us. This is generally what we think about when we think about forgiveness. But Dr. James' research demonstrates that people who practice episodic forgiveness develop something termed trait forgiveness. All this means is that you center forgiveness of others as a fundamental part of how you navigate the world for your own emotional health. They are calmer, have better skills for overcoming obstacles, and are less likely to take the actions of others as personal attacks.

You know how there are just some people out there that seem to human a bit better than most other people? It's not that their lives are golden, it's just that they handle their shit with healthy coping skills and integrity. Those are the people that have integrated trait forgiveness into their personalities. They chug that shit like its emotional electrolytes. Probably because it is. And I can testify that once I realized that my childhood induction into the Temple of Grudge-Holding was of zero help to my adulting, and began letting go of shit on the regular, I started glimpsing a life steeped in trait forgiveness. I'm getting there, and it's been worth the work.

The Forgiveness Process

Forgiveness is a process, not a sudden epiphany moment where everything is resolved in one fell swoop for ever and ever. And understanding that process is an important part of doing the work.

Frameworks for how we get better are a common part of emotional health work. For example, our understanding of the grief process comes from Elizabeth Kubler-Ross' work in the 1970s around the stages of dying, more commonly known as the "five stages of grief." Few good frameworks are conceptualized as linear steps with a single, permanent resolution. Being human is complicated, and our emotional work is like a lifelong game of Chutes and Ladders with far higher stakes.

I view forgiveness as a very similar process of forward movement, backward movement, relapse, and struggle. I was curious if anyone had broken down that process, stage-wise, as we have for grief work and behavior change. I couldn't find anything. There are lists that are called "stages" but they are really more like how-to steps. Which is cool, if you are looking for practical advice on doing forgiveness work. But that work is so individual that tips and exercises are only a starting point to begin the internal conversation we need to have in order to let go of anger and pain. That work happens in stages, rather than being completed in steps. This may sound like semantics but it's really not. Baking a cake is something you do in steps, right? Cream butter and sugar. Sift together dry ingredients. Blend the two. Stuff that happens in stages is more wibbly-wobbly-timey-wimey than that. There are multiple moving parts (because human, not cake) and no specific recipe for completion.

Just like with any other emotional work, there is no finite endpoint in forgiveness. We may end up back in the process at any time, having to work through things yet

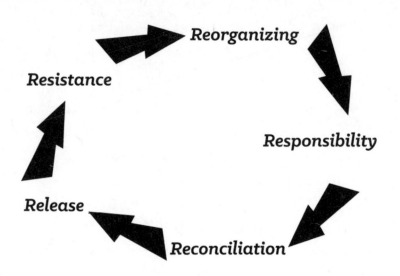

again. And that's OK. It's a fundamental part of the human experience, and of having an overprotective brain that is always remembering the past as an indicator of our possible future.

So I looked at the research on the *process* of forgiveness and created a stage-wise model to help conceptualize how it works. Because knowing where we are and what we are working is incredibly helpful. It normalizes the process when we are feeling frustrated, stuck, and broken. And it gives us a framework for moving forward from those same feelings of frustration, stuckness, and brokenness. It's a reminder that all hard work is a process and that the process is not ever truly complete.

So, first question: why are all the stages alliterative? Well, because when this model becomes famous, it's an accepted clinical practice that will make it easier to memorize for when people are taking the National Counseling Exam. I got you, fam.

Second question: what do you mean by all of these terms? Even better, let's unpack them.

Resistance: This is probably the most self-explanatory part of the model. It's about our own resistance to forgiving someone who has harmed us. If we are holding onto a strong, negative emotion like anger, there is generally a really good reason we have it. It means we were hurt by something quite badly and there is generally a person or persons that hurt us— some fucker caused our suffering. Why would we want to let them off the hook? They deserve our rage, right? Really, "retaliation" should be the appropriate "R" word that we should be using here—I mean, that's what it feels like when we are angry at someone. The idea of letting go of that anger feels counterintuitive to protecting ourselves from more hurt in the future.

Reorganizing: In this stage we start to really process all the parts of the situation. We have to unpack all our shit around it. What was done to us, the hows and whys of the circumstances, what aspects of the situation belong to others and which belong to us. Every situation has context and this stage is when we start realizing that there is far more to the situation than the story we have been telling ourselves about the person or people who hurt us. This may mean reconsidering intent or other outside influences. For example, someone's hurting of you isn't excused because of their own abuse history, but it can really change the context around why they treated you the way they did.

Responsibility: Ok, this is hard shit. This is the process that is so deeply individual there are some decent tools to get you started but no real foolproof hacks. Because this is a conversation between your rational, higher self and your wounded, protected emotional self. And that conversation involves taking responsibility for your own emotional content. I remember calling my mother with some profound butthurt toward a supervisor when I was 18 years old. And in her infinite and no-bullshit wisdom she told me something that I wrote on an index card and hung on my bathroom mirror as a reminder: *They can fuck you over but they* *can't fuck you up.* Others are accountable for their behavior, but the only person accountable for my response is me. That hardly seems fair when people are being truly awful but there is also an extreme freedom in realizing that the one power that no one can take from me in any situation is the power of my own response. Taking responsibility for my own response means taking ownership of my life back. It means untethering myself from a chain of shitty, coercive, or abusive behavior by someone else. There is a real badassery in that.

Reconciliation: Reconciliation is the act of making one thing compatible with another. For those of you old enough to remember check books, we used to reconcile our account, which meant going through our checkbook ledger to make sure what we had on paper matched what was actually in our bank accounts (which we found by looking at our paper statements. So much work!). In this case, we have to reconcile our emotional content with the harmful behaviors we engage in because of it. Even if we aren't taking it out on anyone else, the continued rumination and angry thoughts are hurting *us*, right? And we have to reconcile our actions with our internal moral center . . . with who we know ourselves to be. I haven't met anyone who considers themselves a pissed off, vengeful person. Everyone I have ever talked to considers themselves a peaceful person who just wants to be happy. So we have to reconcile our anger and how we react from it with that internal peaceful person. Being continuously angry is not compatible with being a peaceful person at heart, is it? At least, I haven't figured out a way to do it.

Release: If the other parts seemed hard, this is the absolute *worst*. This is the part of the process where our realization of the mismatch between internal self and continued emotional state requires action. We are hurting ourselves and others. This doesn't mean giving up on working for change if change needs to happen. It definitely doesn't mean you need to let people who hurt you stomp all over you again. It means that the anger that propels you to a response of safety is no longer necessary. It is meant only as an immediate burst of protective energy that is not currently needed. And continuing to hold on to the anger and developing a long term angry mood, serves only a continued source of pain for *us*. Only with releasing that anger, can we truly move on and reconnect with our inner, peaceful nature.

If you are energetically hung up on something from the past, figuring out where you are and making a conscious effort to continue working toward forgiveness is a good start. It's also important not to beat yourself up when you think you're done and moving forward and you notice your anger is stirred up again. There's a reason Buddhist monks do mindful meditation for hours and hours a day for decades and decades and decades . . . learning to proactively respond to our own physiological responses isn't easy, no matter what the love-and-light Instagram gurus tell you. A lot of the exercises in this book are designed to propel the insight needed to propel this process. But there is no alchemical equation to make it happen instantaneously.

All this is to say that forgiveness isn't a one and done thing where you write your grievances on a slip of paper and toss them into a fire and then everything is magically better. And if you *did* do that at some point I'm guessing that you had already been working through the first four stages at some level, and you processed your last stage through ceremony, which is a powerful thing for people. You still did the other work . . . and that's really tough. Give yourself serious credit.

Supporting the Process

So the big question is, how do you do this forgiveness shit if it's so important? Since there is no magic wand and bibbity bobbity boo spell for it, I have no simplistic answer for you. I do know from my own experiences, and the experiences of the clients I have seen work through this process, that there are certain tips that can help you establish your own path to forgiveness.

1) *Feel your anger and your pain, and share that story with someone safe if you haven't already.* Dr. Luskin's research demonstrated that we can't forgive what we haven't acknowledged, therefore doing so is an important part of the process. The phrase *spiritual bypassing* was coined by psychotherapist Dr. Robert Masters (as explained in the book by the same name) to describe using spiritual practices as a way of not coping with our unresolved wounds. Expressions like "Everything happens for a reason" and "There is a greater lesson in this" are examples of spiritual bypassing. I've seen time and again people who think they should not experience their hurt because it meant they weren't good practitioners of a specific religious faith or spiritual path. Meaning if they

are angry they are also bad Christians, Buddhists, Muslims, etc. So in order to walk a spiritual path in the way they feel they are meant to, they stuff their feelings and disavow them versus recognizing them, honoring them, and working through them. Embrace what you are feeling with self-compassion for your experience. You can't forgive what you haven't acknowledged.

2) **Find the helpers and forgivers, not the enablers.** Sharing your story is vital to healing, but it needs to be with the right type of person. Nourishing social support makes all the difference. Studies cited by Dr. Luskin show that early on, people who connect with others who comfort them while helping them cope in healthy ways are far more likely to achieve recovery and forgiveness. You want the people around you who will be honest with you, and you want to act on the feedback they give you. People who let you sit in your grievance story aren't helpful to the process. And if you ignore the people giving you helpful and hopeful advice, you are also far more likely to become stuck. If it's a longer-term pattern of stuckness? Dr. Pert was an advocate for finding people and community in which the process of trait forgiveness is cultural

value. This may be church, or a meditation group, or therapy, whether group or individual. But if you get wrapped up with people who encourage and egg on your anger, you will feed off that vibe. I can testify that being around kind and peaceful people helps me resonate with my kind and peaceful self.

3) **Consider your attribution process.** Dr. Luskin calls this "find the impersonal in your hurt." What he is referring to is something that science calls *fundamental attribution error.* This means we have a tendency to attribute our own behavior as a response to our circumstances, but attribute the behavior of others to the core essence of their badness. So if we cut someone off in traffic, it's because we were distracted and didn't see them, or were anxious because of running late for a big interview, etc. But if someone else cuts us off in traffic, we tend to think it's cuz they suck at being human and don't give a shit about the safety of anyone around them. Western culture exacerbates this tendency. It's one of those operating system bugs of the human brain that we have to locate and patch if we don't want to lose our minds on the regular.

Giving people the benefit of the doubt that they are reacting situationally to the world around them, just as we are, takes the edge off the hurt they cause us. It may not change how we interact with them in the future, or alter the boundaries we establish to shield ourselves from continued hurt, but it can make a *huge* difference in our ability to forgive. Step outside the experience and become curious about it as a social psychologist would. What may have caused their behavior? How did you get caught in the crossfire of *their* pain and anger? When we create a story of grievance, we are creating a *blame hypothesis* that our brain starts grooving on as actual fact, when in reality we don't know for sure. And there may be multiple other hypotheses to work from.

4) **Be specific about what happened to you.** In the Jewish tradition, you can't forgive what someone did to someone else, only what they did to you. My husband's grandmother was a concentration camp survivor in Nazi Germany. He cannot forgive the internment camp officials under the leadership of Adolf Hitler for his grandmother's experiences in the camps. But he can forgive how her experiences affected *his* life. Forgiveness work means releasing our direct connection. If we try to widen our net to forgive the harm experienced by other people, we

get lost in vague complexities that make the work impossible.

5) **Justice has nothing to do with forgiveness.** Legal accountability is separate from forgiveness. It's about what is owed to society for crimes committed, not what is owed to victims. The prosecution of Nazi war crimes after WWII did not change the cascade of epigenetic trauma in my husband's family. It didn't right any wrongs that were committed against his family. The only intent is to stop further harm by the perpetrators. The son of a friend of my family was murdered in a horrific hate crime back in the 1990s. The family petitioned the DA to not pursue the death penalty because having the state murder their son's killer would do nothing to bring them any resolution. The man in question is serving a life sentence and is no longer a danger to queer youth in our community.

6) **Consider the truth of the unenforceability.** Remember the analogy of the stalled cop car, with the cop writing tickets for rules they couldn't enforce? Getting stuck in a pattern of unforgiveness means we want *to enforce rules we are unable to enforce.* In reality, relationships don't come with guarantees. Writing those tickets is the opposite of empowering, constructive action. Focusing on the behavior of others (as rules that should be enforced) keeps us

stuck in helpless rage, and keeps us from being proactive regarding our dealings with them in the present and future. No matter what people "should" or "should not" do or be are not roles that we can force them to comply with.

7) **Don't confuse forgiveness with reconciliation.** Reconciliation means reestablishing a relationship with the person who hurt you. Maybe you want to do that and forgiving them is part of that process. But forgiving someone doesn't mean you are seeking out reconnection. It doesn't mean you go back for more pain. It doesn't make you someone's bitch.

8) **Try a mantra.** One that connects you to forgiveness as a process, not one in which you are trying to rickroll your subconscious into thinking you've already done the work. Dr. Pert has an excellent example in her book *Everything You Need To Know To Feel Good*, and it's simple to remember:

I know that forgiving myself and others for errors of the past allows me to heal.

See how that keeps you mindful of the process and your end goal without pretending you are already there?

9) **Forgive the deed, but remember the lesson**. One of the biggest worries I see with people is that if they

forgive, they will somehow forget. That they will be hurt again by the same person, or by other people in the same ways. As if forgiveness puts a bulls-eye on their chest that declares "go ahead and fuck me over." The reality couldn't be further from the truth. If continued anger is keeping that stress response active in your body, you are constantly in fight-flight-freeze mode. That's a protective mechanism for short-term safety, not a strategic one for long term safety. Don't forget that we are all living in primitive brains and bodies that are not really designed for modern life. It's the reason why chronic states of anger and unforgiveness lead to so many health problems. But forgiveness gets us out of that negative feedback loop and makes us better at holding our boundaries in the future, because we are creating strategies with our thinking brain, not our reactive, protective brain. Forgiveness doesn't make you weak—it reinforces your strength.

10) **Consider trying a formal forgiveness process.** The human brain is hardwired for ceremony. I mentioned Dr. Matt James earlier—his research is on the Hawaiian forgiveness practice of *ho'oponopono*. I've been through ho'oponopono with one of his trainers and found it a very helpful process, related to releasing negative feelings toward someone who had died the previous year. His process is an active one,

that isn't steeped in the spiritual bypassing practices many of us have had inflicted upon us in the past. Fred Luskin's book has other good tools and there are many other intentional practices that can also help, like meditating on your intention and hope to forgive. Writing a letter of forgiveness. Stuff like that. Like I said, there's no magic. But the human brain is so wired for ceremony, doing some kind of structured "work" around the process can be really helpful. As is any process that does conscious forgiveness work like writing a letter or meditating on your desire to forgive and release that ongoing emotional connection.

Unfucking Anger: The Check In

Becoming skillful in the management of our emotions is not a recipe. If it was, we'd all follow the recipe and everyone would have a lovely homemade flan of a calm life. Instead, we have to test a lot of different stuff out and find what works best for us. It's tough work. Took a while to get fucked, takes awhile to get unfucked. Checking in on your progress is really helpful in not getting overwhelmed and dissuaded from continuing to work at it.

- Are you finding yourself more or less activated by situations that would make you angry in the past? Are the differences in the level of anger or the number of instances of anger?

- Are you finding that anger's grip on you is getting tighter or looser?

- Are you finding that you have better skills to navigate your anger than you had in the past?

- Do you believe that you have more control over your emotions than you had in the past?

- Are certain skills becoming easier to access and utilize once you are activated? Do you see the potential for them becoming second nature?

Conclusion

**W**hat's the point of going through all this work and rewiring your brain, unless you have a parole officer that is forcing you to? If people are being dicks they deserve the smack down, right? Why should you try to be nicer, kinder, and more patient?

Well, for yourself.

And you totally knew I was going to say that. The anger is fucking you up way more than them. You deserve to live in a body and brain that feels as calm and peaceful as possible. When you don't let anger fester, if you manage it skillfully, it stops taking over all the time. You just fucking *feel better*. You get less angry overall. You've re-trained your brain to be a little less crazy by not acting crazy every time it sets off a warning flare.

Being less angry doesn't mean you let people walk all over you. Quite the opposite. You are more aware of your boundaries, and enforce them without a hair-trigger response. You stop being mad, because you have insight and awareness into what's safe for you. And you insist on your safety, and the safety of those you love.

Part of not being controlled by your feelings of anger means creating the kinds of relationships in which your boundaries are respected. So you create better relationships. You can be that person that it feels good to be around, the one who is respected but not walked all over.

You know, be the change, and all that shit. It kinda works. Just sayin'.

Bibliography

Affect Regulation and Addictive Aspects of Repetitive Self-Injury in Hospitalized Adolescents. (2010, January 04). Retrieved from https://www.sciencedirect.com/science/article/abs/pii/S0890856709606390

Behavioral Tech, LLC (n.d.). What is DBT? | Behavioral Tech. http://behavioraltech.org/resources/whatisdbt.cfm

Besharat, Mohammad Ali; Nia, Mahin Etemadi; Farahani, Hojatollah. (2013). Anger and major depressive disorder: The mediating role of emotion regulation and anger rumination. Asian Journal of Psychiatry, 6, 35-41.

Carter, L., & Minirth, F. B. (1993). The Anger Workbook. Nashville, TN: Thomas Nelson.

Childhood origins of self-destructive behavior. (1991). American Journal of Psychiatry, 148(12), 1665-1671. doi:10.1176/ajp.148.12.1665

Emerson, D. (2015). Trauma-sensitive yoga in therapy: Bringing the body into treatment. New York: W.W. Norton & Company.

Fava, M., & Rosenbaum, J. F. (1998). Anger attacks in depression. Depression and Anxiety, 8(S1), 59-63. doi:10.1002/(sici)1520-6394(1998)8:1 3.0.co;2-y

Goldstein, David S(Sep 2010) Adrenaline and Noradrenaline. In: eLS. John Wiley & Sons Ltd, Chichester. http://www.els.net [doi: 10.1002/9780470015902.a0001401.pub2]

Harper, F. G. (2018). This is your brain on anxiety: What happens and what helps. Portland, OR: Microcosm Publishing.

Harper, F. G. (2018). This Is Your Brain on Depression. Microcosm Publishing.

Harper, F. G. (2017). Unfuck Your Brain: Using Science to Get over Anxiety, Depression, Anger, Freak-Outs, and Triggers. Microcosm Publishing.

Heider, F. (1958) the psychology of interpersonal relations, New York: Wiley

James, M. (2017). Ho'oponopono: Your path to true forgiveness. Carlsbad, CA: Crescendo Publishing.

Jones, E. E. and Davis, K. E. (1965) From acts to dispositions: the attribution process in social psychology, in L. Berkowitz (ed.), Advances in experimental social psychology (Volume 2, pp. 219-266), New York: Academic Press

Jones, E. E. and Harris, V. A. (1967). The attribution of attitudes. Journal of Experimental Social Psychology, 3, 1-24

Jones, M.B., and Jones, D.R. (1995). Preferred pathways of behavioural contagion. Journal of Psychiatric Research, 29:193-209.

Jones, E. E. and Nisbett, R. E. (1972). The actor and the observer: Divergent perceptions of the causes of the behavior. In E. E. Jones, D. E. Kanouse, H. H. Kelley, R. E. Nisbett, S. Valins and B. Weiner (eds.), Attribution: Perceiving the causes of behavior (pp. 79-94). Morristown, NJ: General Learning Press.

Leahy, R.L., Tirch, D., & Napolitano, L.A. (2011). Emotion Regulation in Psychotherapy: A Practitioner's Guide 1st Edition. The Guilford Press, New York.

Lee, C., & Ghiya, S. (2012). Influence of alternate nostril breathing on heart rate variability in non-practitioners of yogic breathing. International Journal of Yoga, 5(1), 66. doi:10.4103/0973-6131.91717

Lindebaum, D., & Geddes, D. (2015). The place and role of (moral) anger in organizational behavior studies. *Journal of organizational behavior*, *37*(5), 738–757. doi:10.1002/job.2065

LUSKIN, F. (2016). FORGIVE FOR GOOD. New York, NY: HARPERONE.

Mohan, R., Jain, S., & Ramavat, M. R. (2015). Effect of Alternate Nostril Breathing on Cardiovascular Parameters in Obese Young Adults. International Journal of Physiology, 3(1), 108. doi:10.5958/2320-608x.2015.00024.4

Mohanty, S. (2016). Comments on "Alternate Nostril Breathing at Different Rates and Its Influence on Heart Rate Variability in Non Practitioners of Yoga". Journal Of Clinical And Diagnostic Research. doi:10.7860/jcdr/2016/20276.8145

Patel, A. (2017, August 10). When anxiety turns into anger, experts say you shouldn't ignore it. Retrieved from https://globalnews.ca/news/3654939/anxiety-and-anger/

Perry, J. C., & Cooper, S. H. (1986). A Preliminary Report on Defenses and Conflicts Associated with Borderline Personality Disorder. *Journal of the American Psychoanalytic Association, 34*(4), 863-893. doi:10.1177/000306518603400405

Pert, C. B., & Marriot, N. (2007). Everything you need to know to feel good. London: Hay House.

Plowden, Keith O.; Adams, Linda Thompson; Wiley, Dana. (2016). Black and blue: Depression and African American men. Archives of Psychiatric Nursing, 30, 630-635.

Preidt, R. (n.d.). Depression May Be Worse When Accompanied by Anger, Irritability – WebMD. Retrieved from https://www.webmd.com/depression/news/20130911/depression-may-be-worse-when-accompanied-by-anger-irritability

Rao U. DSM-5: disruptive mood dysregulation disorder. *Asian J Psychiatr.* 2014;11:119–123. doi:10.1016/j.ajp.2014.03.002

Rosellini, G., & Worden, M. (1985). Of Course You're Angry. United States of America: Hazeldon.

Ross, L. (1977) The intuitive psychologist and his shortcomings: Distortions in the attribution process. In L. Berkowitz (ed.), Advances in experimental social psychology (Volume 10, pp. 173-240), Orlando, FL: Academic Press

Ross, L, Amabile, T. M. and Steinmetz, J. L.(1977) Social roles, social control and biases in social perception, Journal of Personality and Social Psychology, 35, 485-494

Ross, L., Lepper, M. R. and Hubbard, M. (1975) Perseverance in self-perception and social perception: Biased attributional processes in the debriefing paradigm, Journal of Personality and Social Psychology, 32, 880-892

Safer DJ. Irritable mood and the Diagnostic and Statistical Manual of Mental Disorders. *Child Adolesc Psychiatry Ment Health.* 2009;3(1):35. Published 2009 Oct 24. doi:10.1186/1753-2000-3-35

Sahu, A., Gupta, P., & Chatterjee, B. (2014). Depression is more than just sadness: A case of excessive anger and its management in depression. Indian Journal of Psychological Medicine, 36(1), 77. doi:10.4103/0253-7176.127259

Segal, Z.V., Williams, M., Teasdale, J.D., 2002. Mindfulness-based Cognitive Therapy for Depression: A New Approach to Preventing Relapse. Guildford Publications, New York.

Self-injury (Cutting, Self-Harm or Self-Mutilation). (2016, August 17). Retrieved from http://www.mentalhealthamerica.net/self-injury

Singh, N. N., Lancioni, G. E., Singh, S. D., Winton, A. S. W., Sabaawi, M., Wahler, R. G., & Singh, J. (2007). Adolescents with conduct disorder can be mindful of their aggressive behavior. Journal of Emotional and Behavioral Disorders, 15(1), 56-63.

Teasdale, J.D., Segal, Z.V., Williams, J.M.G., Ridgeway, V.A., Soulsby, J.M., Lau, M.A., 2000. Prevention of relapse/recurrence in major depression by mindfulness based cognitive therapy. Journal of Consulting and Clinical Psychology, 68, 615–623.

Weisinger, H. (1985). Dr. Weisinger's Anger workout book. New York: Quill.

Whitlock, J.L., Exner-Cortens, D. & Purington, A. (under review). Validity and reliability of the non-suicidal self-injury assessment test (NSSI-AT)

UNF#CK YOUR BRAIN

GETTING OVER ANXIETY, DEPRESSION, ANGER, FREAK-OUTS, AND TRIGGERS...WITH SCIENCE!

FAITH G. HARPER, PHD, LPC-S, ACS

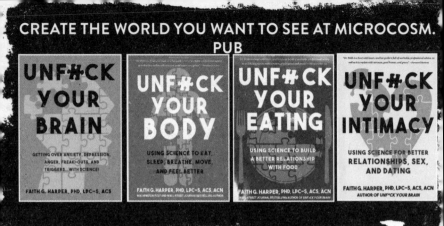